LET'S FIND OUT! EARTH SCIENCE

WHAT ARE RIVERS, LAKES, AND OCEANS?

LOUISE SPILSBURY

ROSEN
EDUCATIONAL SERVICES

Published in 2014 by Britannica Educational Publishing (a trademark of Encyclopædia Britannica, Inc.) in association with The Rosen Publishing Group, Inc.
29 East 21st Street, New York, NY 10010

Distributed exclusively by Rosen Publishing.
To see additional Britannica Educational Publishing titles, go to rosenpublishing.com

First Edition

Britannica Educational Publishing
J.E. Luebering: Director, Core Reference Group
Anthony L. Green: Editor, Compton's by Britannica

Rosen Publishing
Hope Lourie Killcoyne: Executive Editor
Nelson Sá: Art Director

Library of Congress Cataloging-in-Publication Data

Spilsbury, Louise.
What are rivers, lakes, and oceans?/Louise Spilsbury.
        pages cm. — (Let's find out: earth science)
Includes bibliographical references and index.
ISBN 978-1-62275-281-2 (library binding) — ISBN 978-1-62275-284-3 (pbk.) — ISBN 978-1-62275-285-0 (6-pack)
1. Oceanography — Juvenile literature. 2. Hydrology — Juvenile literature. I. Title.
JUV GC21.5.S67 2014
551.48 — dc23
                                                                        2013023013

Manufactured in the United States of America

Photo credits
Cover: Shutterstock: R McIntyre. Inside: Dreamstime: Anacoimbra 20, Mrallen 19; Shutterstock: Constantine Androsoff 28, Rob Barklamb 13, S.Borisov 18–19, Eric Broder Van Dyke 15, Devy 29, Frontpage 6–7, Francois Gagnon 11, Josef Hanus 21, Ben Heys 17, Cindy Hughes 5, Im Perfect Lazybones 9, Jiggo the kop 16, Frank L Junior 23, Pierre Leclerc 12, Maksimilian 27, Mikhail Markovskiy 14, R McIntyre 1, Nik Merkulov 4, Fabien Monteil 27, Procy 8, Theeraphol 25, Upthebanner 7, Jaromir Urbanek 10, Michael J. Walters 22, Xonovets 24.

Contents

BLUE PLANET

Viewed from space, Earth looks mostly blue with
scattered brown patches. That is because almost
three-quarters of Earth's surface is covered in water.
Less than one percent of this water is freshwater that
we can drink and use. The rest is mostly saltwater
in the oceans and some is frozen
at the North and South Poles.

Can you see
why people call Earth
the blue planet?

Water in the oceans makes up nearly 98 percent of all the water on Earth.

THINK ABOUT IT

While you read this book, think about how rivers, lakes, and oceans are connected.

We cannot drink seawater because it has so much salt in it. Instead of quenching our thirst, seawater would dry us out. The body tries to get rid of salt by making us produce more urine. If the body loses too much water, it can no longer work.

RIVERS

A river is a large area of moving freshwater. Rivers flow toward oceans, lakes, or other rivers. Some are full of water all year round, but rivers in dry countries may flow only at certain times of year. Some rivers are only a few miles long. Others, such as the Nile in Africa and the Amazon in South America, are so long they flow through many countries.

COMPARE AND CONTRAST

How do the rivers pictured in this book look alike? How do they look different?

▶▶ **The Nile is 4,132 miles (6,650 km) long.**

6

The city of New York developed along the Hudson River.

Rivers are very important to people. In the earliest times, people made their homes alongside rivers so they had freshwater to drink, to wash in, and to cook with. They also caught fish to eat from the river. When people built ships, they used the rivers to travel, explore, and to buy and sell goods from farther inland.

RIVER'S SOURCE

Most rivers start high in hills and mountains as a tiny trickle of water. The start of a river is called its source. A river's source can be falling rain, melting snow, a lake from which a stream flows, or a spring that bubbles up from underground. As the trickle runs downhill, it combines with other trickles, collecting more water from rain and streams along the way.

Trickles of water combining with other trickles may be called a stream, a brook, or a creek.

The water at the top of a river can be powerful and fast-moving.

From its source, a river flows downhill. It moves quickly, and the water can be heavy and powerful. As the water rushes along, it picks up stones and soil from the bottom of the river. Gradually, as it travels, the water cuts riverbeds and carves V-shaped valleys into the land it passes over.

Valleys are deep grooves in the land, carved by rivers.

RIVER STAGES

As rivers reach flatter land, they slow down. Other streams and rivers flow into the main river, making it wider. As the water begins to flow more slowly, it loses power. The river cuts less deeply into the land, and it cannot rush over obstacles such as areas of very hard rock. Instead, the river has to flow around them.

Some rivers flow from side to side in loops and bends called meanders.

THINK ABOUT IT

Why do you think river mouths are home to big fish and other animals that eat small fish?

The mouth of a river is where it empties into a bigger river, a lake, or an ocean. Many towns and cities are built at river mouths because these are good places from which to trade and travel. There are also many fish there, because river water washes small fish into lakes and seas.

What Is a Lake?

A lake is an area of water surrounded by land. Water in a lake is still and does not flow. Lakes form where there is a hole in the land and water to fill it. Some lakes form in the large pits called craters at the top of old volcanoes. Rain falls and fills the space, forming a lake.

Crater Lake in Oregon is a lake that formed at the top of an old volcano.

COMPARE AND CONTRAST
How are lakes and rivers similar? How are they different?

Lakes in the Lake District, England, were formed by glaciers.

Some lakes were formed by glaciers. Glaciers are slowly moving rivers of ice. As giant glaciers moved, they carved out basins and valleys in the land. Later, the ice melted. Some of this water collected in the holes, forming lakes.

People dig out land to make lakes, too. These are called reservoirs. Reservoirs catch and store water that can be pumped to towns and cities for people to use.

LAKES OF THE WORLD

Lakes can be large or small. The highest large lake in the world is Lake Titicaca in South America. It was formed by melted ice and snow filling a hollow in the Andes Mountains. Lake Baikal in Siberia is the deepest, oldest lake in the world.

Siberia's Lake Baikal is believed to be 1 mile (1.6 km) deep.

Some lakes contain salty water. Lakes become salty if their water never drains away. River water that flows into these lakes is fresh, but carries salts from the rocks it flows over. As water evaporates from the lake, the salts stay behind. Over many thousands of years, the salts build up and make the lake water salty rather than fresh.

Parts of the Great Salt Lake in Utah are eight times saltier than the oceans!

When water **evaporates** it becomes warmer, dries up, and changes into water vapor.

CHANGING LAKES

Once formed, lakes do not stay the same. Most lakes last only for a few thousand years. They slowly disappear because when streams and rivers carry water into a lake, they bring sand, small rocks, and soil, too. This sediment settles on the bottom of the lake and, as it builds up, it gradually fills up the lake. This makes the lake shallower and shallower, until it disappears.

Lakes are lost when they fill up with sand, soil, and rocks.

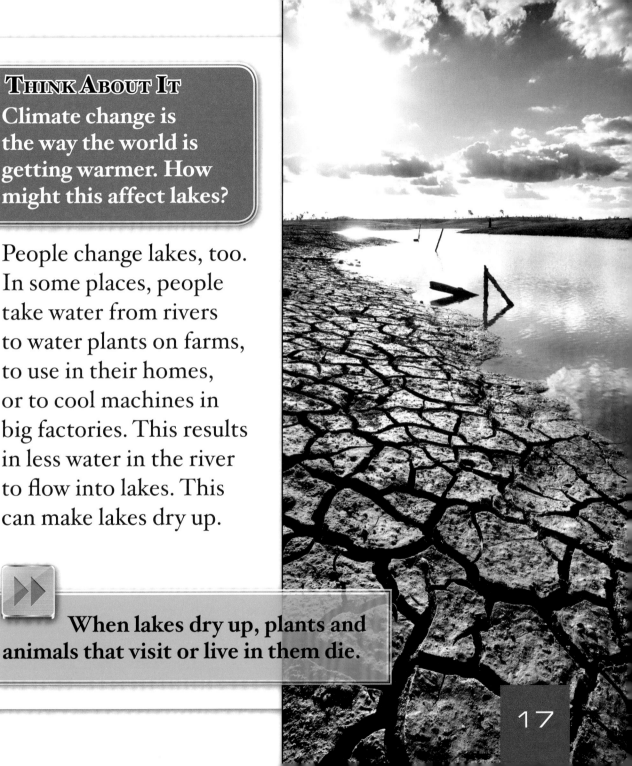

Think About It
Climate change is the way the world is getting warmer. How might this affect lakes?

People change lakes, too. In some places, people take water from rivers to water plants on farms, to use in their homes, or to cool machines in big factories. This results in less water in the river to flow into lakes. This can make lakes dry up.

When lakes dry up, plants and animals that visit or live in them die.

OCEANS

An ocean is a huge body of salt water. There are four main oceans in the world: the Pacific, the Indian, the Atlantic, and the Arctic. These oceans are joined and water is always moving within and between them. One reason water moves between and in the oceans is that when strong winds blow across their surface, they create waves.

THINK ABOUT IT
All the oceans are joined, so why do you think the world changed when people began to build ocean-going ships?

▶▶ The Pacific Ocean is the world's biggest ocean. It covers more of Earth's surface than all the dry land put together.

A special ship called an icebreaker pushes through sea ice in the Arctic Ocean.

Parts of the Arctic Ocean are always frozen into ice. The Arctic Ocean is the smallest, shallowest, and coldest ocean in the world. In the Arctic Ocean there are huge blocks of floating ice, up to 160 miles (257 km) wide!

OCEAN WATERS

Most of the water in the oceans is carried there by rivers. Some water enters oceans by seeping up out of the ground or falling into oceans as rain. The place where freshwater from rivers meets and mixes with the salty water of the ocean is called an estuary.

Plants growing in estuaries have to grow in saltwater and freshwater.

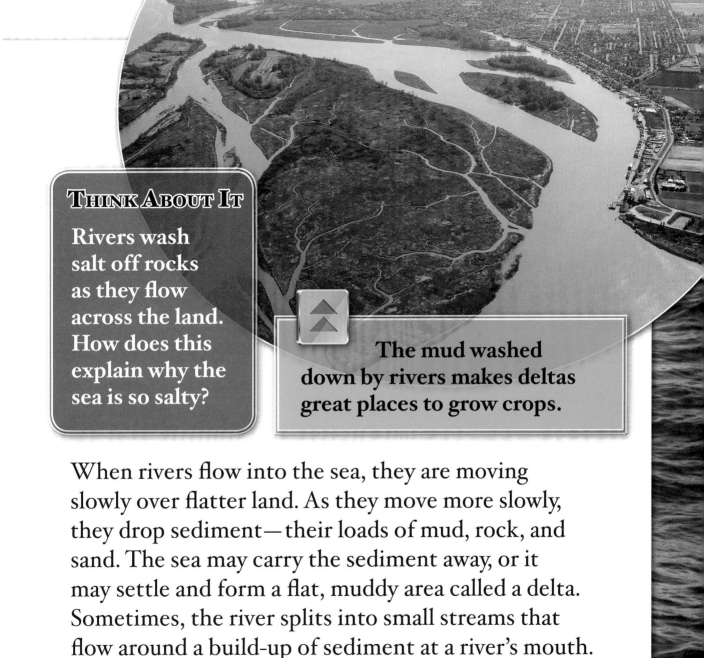

THINK ABOUT IT

Rivers wash salt off rocks as they flow across the land. How does this explain why the sea is so salty?

The mud washed down by rivers makes deltas great places to grow crops.

When rivers flow into the sea, they are moving slowly over flatter land. As they move more slowly, they drop sediment—their loads of mud, rock, and sand. The sea may carry the sediment away, or it may settle and form a flat, muddy area called a delta. Sometimes, the river splits into small streams that flow around a build-up of sediment at a river's mouth.

Tides

In most parts of the world, seawater gradually rises and then falls on the shores where the oceans meet the land. These movements are called tides.

Tides happen throughout the day. There are two high tides and two low tides. High tide is when the sea reaches its highest point up the coast. Low tide is when it has flowed all the way out again.

At high tide, the beach is covered in water.

Tides happen because of the moon's gravity. Earth is spinning all the time. As it turns, the moon's gravity pulls at the oceans nearest to it. This makes the water rise and causes a high tide. Six hours later, Earth has turned 90 degrees. The place where there was a high tide no longer directly faces the moon, and a low tide sets in.

At low tide, there is less water on the beach.

Gravity is the force that pulls on things.

OCEAN DEPTHS

Most of the living things in an ocean are found near the water's surface. That is because the deeper the water, the darker and colder it is. At the surface, tiny plants use sunlight to make their own food. Tiny animals then eat these plants, and other sea animals eat them.

THINK ABOUT IT

Why do you think it gets darker and colder the deeper you go in an ocean?

▶▶ **Plankton are tiny plants and animals that float near the surface of oceans and other bodies of water.**

In some places, underwater mountains are so high they appear above the water as islands.

The ground at the bottom of the ocean may be dark, but it is not completely flat. There are huge, flat areas of ground covered in sand, but there are also high mountains that jut up from the sea floor. There are deep valleys, or cracks, in the ground called trenches, too. In fact, the deepest valleys and tallest mountains in the world are found under the sea!

Pollution

People pollute rivers, lakes, and oceans all over the world. Farmers use sprays and powders on their fields to help crops grow and to kill bugs that harm the plants. Rain can wash these sprays into rivers and streams. In some places, dirty water from bathrooms and kitchens is flushed into rivers, lakes, and seas.

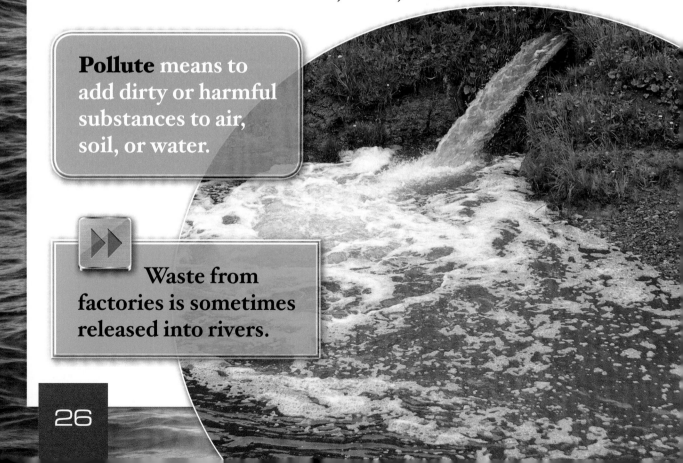

Pollute means to add dirty or harmful substances to air, soil, or water.

▶▶ Waste from factories is sometimes released into rivers.

Polluted water can be harmful to living things. Some animals die when they mistake litter for food. For example, turtles often mistake plastic bags in the sea for jellyfish, and choke when they eat the bags. Polluting water also reduces the amount of clean, freshwater people can use.

THINK ABOUT IT

How do you think pollution poured into rivers gets into lakes and oceans?

Some of the litter that gets into the oceans washes back onto beaches.

Using Water

We need to protect rivers, lakes, and oceans because we rely on water in many different ways. People lose at least 3 pints (1.4 l) of water every day through body processes, such as sweating. We must drink plenty of water to replace the water that we lose. We also use moving water in rivers to turn machines that make electricity.

People build huge dams, such as this one, to collect water. The water then rushes through pipes to turn machines that make electricity.

Transport is just one of the many ways we use water!

We use water for washing, cooking, and cleaning. We catch fish and other foods from rivers, lakes, and oceans. We use water to grow plants. Farmers give water to animals to drink so they can provide us with milk, eggs, and meat. We swim, sail, and surf, in rivers, lakes, and oceans, and enjoy them in other ways, too.

THINK ABOUT IT

How important is water to life on Earth? What would happen without it?

29

GLOSSARY

climate change The increase in Earth's temperature caused partly by people burning fuels such as coal and oil.

crater A hollow cavity shaped like a bowl around the opening of a volcano.

delta A fan-shaped piece of land made by deposits of mud and sand at the mouth of a river.

freshwater Water that comes from rivers and lakes. Freshwater is not salty.

glaciers Slow-moving bodies of ice.

ice The solid form of water. Water turns into ice when it gets so cold it freezes.

icebreaker A special type of ship that can push through ocean ice.

meanders Parts of a river or stream that flow in loops and bends around an obstacle.

mouth The end of a river, where it flows into a bigger river, a lake, or an ocean.

obstacles Things that are in the path of a river.

Poles The two points at opposite ends of Earth, the North Pole and South Pole.

reservoirs Lakes made by people to catch and store water to later use.

sea A great body of salty water not as large as an ocean, such as the Mediterranean Sea.

sediment Tiny pieces of rock, mud, or sand.

source The start of a river.

spring The place where water from under the ground comes out onto land.

tides The gradual rise and fall of seawater on the shore where the oceans meet the land.

urine Waste material that is secreted by the kidneys.

volcanoes Holes in Earth's surface from which hot, melted rock called lava can spurt.

water vapor When water is a gas in the air. Water comes in three states: water vapor (gas), water (liquid water), and ice (solid water).

FOR MORE INFORMATION

Books

Berger Kaye, Cathryn, Philippe Cousteau, and EarthEcho International. *Make a Splash!: A Kid's Guide to Protecting Our Oceans, Lakes, Rivers, & Wetlands*. Minneapolis, MN: Free Spirit Publishing, 2012.

Gosman, Gillian. *What Do You Know About Earth's Oceans?* (20 Questions: Earth Science). New York, NY: Powerkids Press, 2013.

MacQuitty, Miranda. *Ocean* (DK Eyewitness Books). New York, NY: DK Publishing, 2008.

Simon, Seymour. *Oceans*. New York, NY: Harper Collins, 2006.

Waldron, Melanie. *Rivers* (Habitat Survival). North Mankato, MN: Raintree, 2013.

Websites

Due to the changing nature of Internet links, Rosen Publishing has developed an online list of Websites related to the subject of this book. This site is updated regularly. Please use this link to access the list:

http://www.rosenlinks.com/lfo/river

Index